JuAnna and the Sad Little Bubble Fairy

Copyright © 2021 by Patricia McLaughlin.

ISBN-978-1-955691-38-3 (sc)
ISBN-978-1-955691-39-0 (hc)
ISBN-978-1-955691-20-8 (eBook)

All rights reserved. No part of this book may be reproduced or transmitted in any form or by any means, electronic or mechanical, including photocopying, recording, or by any information storage and retrieval system, without permission in writing from the copyright owner.

The views expressed in this work are solely those of the author and do not necessarily reflect the views of the publisher, and the publisher hereby disclaims any responsibility for them.

Matchstick Literary
1-888-306-8885
orders@matchliterary.com

Jimmy and Bonnie

You both found your wings too early in life, yet will never be forgotten. Please continue to light up our stars at night and send us many rainbows after the storms.

Down in the valley where all the flowers grow
are the Bubble Fairies sitting all in a row.
They flutter here, they flutter there,
they flutter everywhere,
Their laughter fills the sunny skies
as they fly without a care.

On this fine day, the Bubble Fairies
were soaring round and round.
All of them, except for one, who
was crawling on the ground.
"What's wrong my friend", they did ask
as they held her little hand.
"Why don't you fly about with us?
Why crawl upon the land?"

Now, Lilli looked at her friends
with big tears in her eyes,
She told them all the reason that
she could no longer fly.
The fairies were so very sad as Lilli spoke to them
while sitting on a wooden log with her special friends

They felt so bad and hopeless, and
then an idea came to them
"We know someone who can help,
someone we call our friend."
They start looking for that special
friend as they flutter all about,
then they see JuAnna and they give a joyful shout.

Now JuAnna loves the fairies, each and every one.
She loves them mostly when they
all sparkle in the sun.
They look so very colorful as they
spread their wings to fly.
They soar way up toward the
clouds; way up into the sky.

Their wings begin to flutter as the Bubble Fairies smile;
They fly right to JuAnna to stay with her a while.
JuAnna saw that there was one
who looked so very sad.
She had a frown upon her face;
she was feeling rather bad.

Juanna held out her hands and
this fairy crawled to her,
She looked into JuAnna's eyes as
her's filled up with tears.
"What's wrong little one," JuAnna
said, "You look so sad today.
Sit here and talk to me a bit while
the other fairies play."

Lilli looked at JuAnna and gave a hopeless sigh.
Then, she began a tale so sad that
it made her start to cry.
"When I woke up this morning, I felt a little strange.
I was not sure what it was, but I
knew that I had changed.

I looked into the mirror and then to my surprise,
The problem was right there ….right before my eyes.

My wings were gone; they no longer
shined in the bright sunlight.
"I looked all about but they had
just vanished in the night."

Lilli cried even harder as she told her tale of woe.
She looked at JuAnna as the tears
just flowed and flowed.
"I've always had my wings, it's true,"
Lilli said with a big frown;
"Today they're gone I cannot fly; I'm
stuck here on the ground.
They're really gone, they disappeared;
I don't know what to do,
I cannot fly I can only crawl, just as I did to you."

JuAnna looked at her friend as love
flowed from her heart.
She knew she had to help Lilli find her special part.

"I know you lost your special wings,
but please don't sit and cry.
If instead we think and look we
will find them by and by."

Lilli stopped her crying and listened to what she heard,
She thought, "JuAnna is very smart
so I'll listen to her words."
JuAnna looked left to right as she began to think.
"Did you look in the fountain where
birds go to get a drink?"

Lilli stopped, shook her head, and then began to stare.
Then she said quite happily, "I'm sure they are in there."
She quickly crawled across the lawn
to that little water dish,

She glanced inside...but all she saw
was one tiny golden fish.

"What about behind that rock, sitting on the ground?"
Lilli looked about and said, "That's
where they will be found!"
Lilli crawled very quickly to the
rock by the old brown tree
She was absolutely sure that's
where her wings would be.
But when she looked behind that rock,
there was nothing on the ground,
Except a tiny, slimy worm crawling all around.

Then JuAnna said "behind that tree,
I think that's where your wings will be."
Lilli said, "I'll look and see if my
wings right there could be."
Yet, when quickly behind that tree she glanced,
all she saw was a bunch of busy, red ants.

As Lilli looked at JuAnna, her very special friend,
tears began to fill her eyes and
she started to cry again.
"We've looked around and around,
they simply are not here,"
and down her face crawled another
"bubble-fairy" tear.

JuAnna then remembered a treasure she had found;
It was a special penny just sitting on the ground.
She reached into her pocket and
held that coin up high;
It shined just like those fairies
soaring high up in the sky.

JuAnna said to Lilli as she knelt upon one knee,
"Dry those eyes, here's a coin, it's magical you'll see".
Over there's a wishing well just toss this penny in,
And soon you'll get a big surprise that
will surely make you grin."

Lilli wasn't sure that JuAnna's words were true,
but she decided to do what JuAnna said to do.
She took that special penny and tossed it way up high,
It twisted round and round, then
dropped out of the sky.

Deep into that wishing well that coin found its way,
while Lilli closed her big, green eyes as she began to say,
"Oh, wishing well please help me find my wings somewhere,
I want to stop this crawling and soar up in the air."

Suddenly it happened right there and then that day,
Lilli's wings returned to her in a very special way.
They popped right out on her back
and were shining oh so bright
Lilli was so happy; everything was finally right.

"Thank You JuAnna for your help,
a special friend you are,
and now that I have my wings I can fly so very far".
Happily, she soared up high to join her fairy friends,
This tale of Lilli and her lost wings is coming to an end

THEN.....

Lilli returned to that well and sat upon the edge,
"Thank You, Thank You, Oh So Much"
was all that Lilli said.

Dedication

I would like to dedicate this book to my many newly-founded grandchildren, nieces and nephews, who have inspired me in many ways that even they cannot imagine. Madilyn Cancro, Emily, Natalie and Stephanie Ahern, Julia Wade, Isabella Gillette, Angelica, Anthony, Olivia Molligi, Libby, Logan, Leo IV Redding, Angel and Anthony Warf, and Aubrey and Aiden Redding; to all of you I say a heartfelt "thanks". Thank you also to Reilly and Marissa Quinn who have always been a very important part of my extended family. Vincent and Brianna Caccamesi may be newer additions but are a welcomed part as well. I must also add to this list my "adopted grandchildren" Madden and Morgan Yost who have welcomed my books as a part of their library for the past few years and never found a reason to correct them in any way. You all know the value of having those "special wings." Sometimes your "wings" are right before your eyes, to find them you just have to search within yourself. Then, once you find them never let them go, as they will always be your guide in life. Finally, fill all your gardens with rows of flowers and you'll always love life for what it is.

Acknowledgement

I would like to acknowledge my children and their mates: Jamie and Jen, Jenni, Heidi and Jose, Erin and Bob, Mandy, Sean, and Tim, for your continued support and praise for my books. If ever I falter in the belief that another book can be published, you all come along and boost me up again. I would also like to add to this list my forever cheerleaders: Kayla, Dave, Haley, Cody, Alyssa, Tori, Mason and Briella, and last but not least Juliana who lights up this book in every way. I am proud to introduce you all as my legacy, and no one is richer than me right now. I would like to add a special "thank you" to Jenny Zhu for her beautiful illustrations once again

About The Author

Pat McLaughlin lives in Lowell, Massachusetts where she has resided most of her life. She is also the author of *Two Little Farmers in One Wooden Shoe, Lissi Anne and the Isle of the Gumdrop Trees, Fuzzy Learns a Lesson of Love,* and *The Children of Vaaylor.* While her books are fictitious in nature, they are all based on the antics of the children who surround her. As she goes through life, her stories will continue to come alive through her words and the illustrations as these children give her reasons to laugh and enjoy life every day.

About the Illustrator

Jenny Zhu is a Junior who goes to high school in San Diego, California. She has been drawing ever since she was able to hold a pencil, and her love for art inspired her to become a published illustrator. Jenny hopes to brighten people's days by taking them on a journey inside the whimsical worlds of storybooks through her colorful artworks. She aspires to kindle the imaginative minds of children and young artists out there to explore the boundless depths of their own creativity. Her dream is to pursue art and computer science at Stanford University, and her goals in life are to own an art shop and travel the world. Jenny is also the illustrator of another of Pat Mclaughlin's books, *The Children of Vaaylor*.

www.ingramcontent.com/pod-product-compliance
Lightning Source LLC
Chambersburg PA
CBHW041100070526
44579CB00002B/19